The Fall and Other Poems

The Fall
& Other Poems

J. Bottum

St. Augustine's Press
South Bend, Indiana
2001

Manufactured in the United States of America.

1 2 3 4 5 6 07 06 05 04 03 02 01

Library of Congress Cataloging in Publication Data
Bottum, J.
    The fall & other poems / J. Bottum.
      p. cm.
    ISBN 1-58731-250-6 (alk. paper)
    1. Christian poetry, American. I. Title: Fall and other poems. II. Title.
PS3602.O886 F3 2001
811'.6 – dc21   2001004046

∞ *The paper used in this publication meets the minimum requirements of the American National Standard for Information Sciences – Permanence of Paper for Printed Materials, ANSI Z39.48-1984.*

Contents

V

VI

VII

VIII

Acknowledgments

"Restoration" appeared in *Books & Culture* and "Modern Catholic Verse" in *Crisis*. The following poems were published in the journal *First Things*: "Baptism," "Black Scrawl," "The Boston School of Beauty," "Diaspora," "Dirge," "The Fall," "Fiat Rex," "In Refusal of Politics," "The Undivided Heart," "Timor Mortis," "The Winter Orchard."

Many of these poems were born from conversations, about poetry and much else, which the other participants perhaps little remember, but which precipitated something in me that eventually became these pages. Thanks are thus due Margaret Boerner, Midge Decter, Stan DeTurris, David and Danielle Frum, Dana Gioia, René Girard, Heather Hyde, Leon Kass, William Kristol, Russell Hittinger, Neal Kozodoy, the late Thomas McTighe, Fr. Richard John Neuhaus, Michael Novak, Jim Piercey, Richard Starr, and Norman Wells. Thanks are also owed Matthew Berke, Bryan Crockett, James Nuechterlein, Laurance Wieder, John Wilson, and Claudia Winkler, all of whom contributed their criticism and friendship.

This collection could easily be dedicated to them all, but I long ago promised it to the only true begetter, my wife Lorena: *Fortitudo et decor indumentum eius*, as it says in Proverbs 31:25, *et ridebit in die novissimo*.

I

Baptism

Since the cold sea first learned to speak in tongues
and howled aghast at its madman's chains,
since the Eden break, since the winterspring,
since the star-aspired spires rained
back to earth with stone disdain,
who's thanked the Lord for broken things?

Down the babbled days that brook no praise
or blame – no everlast, no stay –
the brutal waters waste to bless:
the transubstantial stones decay,
the solid monstrance wears away.
Nothing is its inwardness.

The greenhill blood the green heart beats,
even this at last must cease.
From the sudden shade, from the owl light,
a sparrow falls and falling, dies.
The blood tide dims. Dark waters rise
till lowered sky and lakeshore meet

and all things fade: this pine, this tree,
this life, this scene, this *this* – now not.
And yet, not not. In dark, we see:
nothing's found where nothing's sought,
in silence is the silence caught,
and still breath moves the unmoving sea.

Restoration

There were words fit for love – love's words:
shy commoners to bow abashed,
sly courtiers and favored fools,
tongue's pets indulged for prettiness,
blood princes, dukes, to stand on rank,
and kings – yes, even monarch speech
commanding heart's obedience
in beauty's due and measured state.

It was in spring, the lilac blown,
the Judas thorn, that I went mad.
Our civil kingdom's come undone.
Buttocks, bellies, breasts, eyes.
Speechless tongues and mouths turned down.
Beneath the apple dress I saw
wet petals white on nameless thighs,
the wanton swell, disorder's rage –

Was this when words began to fail?
Noon trulls, slick merds, the cancered dogs,
the rags, the clotted graves: our speech
is shoddy-stuffed with winding sheets.
Vows penny-dozen, nothing down.
Mud streets of jabber, sudden, cheap.
The dull pretenders tramping south.
The mute insurgents coiling hate.

It was in fall I saw her face
above the hedge. An order rose.
We walked among the clean-swept courts,
the crowns of marigold, the rue,

the blush and spark of words made new.
Love is lust to meaning wed.
I saw the apple trees grow red
with fruit and gardens bright with leaves.

Timor Mortis

Death is the night watch   death is the waker,
The waiter, the wanter   the watcher of sleep.
Death is the break   death is the breaker,
The wake of the sleeping   the waking of sleep.

Down in the hole   the creaker is turning.
Down in the hole   he starts up awake.
The frost on his fingers   cracks in his yearning.
The blood of the sparrow   streaks on his face.

The flinch of the doe   as she drinks at the river,
The twitch of the owl   the flutter of mice:
Death is the sudden   shrill in the shiver,
The shudder, the stutter   the stand-still of night.

Down in the hole   the hunger is calling,
The belly, the bone-home   the empty of earth.
Down in the hole   the sleeper is falling:
The clutch of the bellman   the bringer to church.

Death is the night watch   death is the waker,
The waiter, the wanter   the watcher of sleep.
Death is the break   death is the breaker,
The wake of the sleeping   the waking of sleep.

The Libertine against Abortion
(after Ovid, *Amores* 2.13)

My rash Corinna lies near death,
her belly bleeding from the life she wrenched away.
    Stupid, stupid girl – your breath
should bear the dueling cries of love, not lonely pain.
    I'd spank you if I had you near:
across my knee, switch back your skirt . . . O foolish girl,
    my anger falls before my fear
that I will lose your golden skin, your laughing eyes,
    your kiss, your arch, your sigh, your fold.
And I'm to blame you felt the spring of life within –
    or so, at least, I'm forced to hold:
What has sufficient cause we must conceive as so.
    Desire only desire sates,
my ripe Corinna, what did you expect? Perfection
    overflows, and love creates
itself in recreation. Your fresh life aroused
    the life in me, and life – refreshed –
came back to you. How could we reject the gift
    we labored for while our lives meshed?
O Goddess of Birth, Ilithyia, who comforts women
    through the pain that makes life new,
forgive the girl who tried to flee from your embrace,
    and sparing her, thus spare me too.
I'll fill your shrine with votive gifts inscribed "For Life."
    I'll kneel before your altar's door
contrite – with virgin oil and fertile grain – to vow
    that when she's well, we'll try once more.

The Spring Advances
(after Horace, *Odes* 4.7)

Against the snow, the spring advances: fields and trees
parade like green recruits.
Winter's armies melt away, and past its flood
the raging stream recedes.

Now the shameless goddess joins her laughing nymphs
to toy in peaceful waters.
The blush of setting sun reminds us not to look
for days that have no end:

Winter wastes away in warming winds and spring
is trampled down by summer,
flagging autumn spends her strength in fruit and slow
winter then resumes.

But seasons know the turning year will soon return them.
When you and I are set
down to sleep with dusty kings, our tethered shadows
spring and fall no more.

Who knows the sum of unspent time or thinks the gods
will loan an extra day?
Only what we squander for ourselves escapes
the clutch of anxious heirs.

Once we drop below the west and eyeless judges
carve their stone decrees,
not righteousness nor noble birth nor skill with words
restores our day to light.

Chaste Diana cannot break her grave lover
from the clasp of darkness,
nor from his chains will mourning Theseus recall
his cold, forgetful friend.

The Fall

I. September

New England comes to flower dying.
Leaves like broken petals trail
in fluttered rage from tainted trees.
        The year grows willful. Stagnant ponds
strain to clamber quarry walls.
Time slips indenture, backing age
        on fuddled age, confusing fall
with summer – snow with hawthorn flurries,
apple flakes along black boughs.
        North of Boston, fire falls
from tree to tree, and leaf by leaf
perverse New England springs to bloom.
        The world is kindling for the Lord.
Sour births and welcome slaughters,
gravid fathers getting sons,
        eastern sunsets, maddened mothers,
brazen midnights, talking dogs,
blood and spew and mongerings of war:
        I woke to see New England burning,
woke to see September's flames
streaming like the blood of martyrs
        guttered in the towns of Maine.
I watched the woods of Concord catch,
the flash of Canaan, Bethel, Keene,
        the angry hills of Holyoke.
The forests of Vermont have gained
for Boston not a single day
        and all the trees of Plymouth rise
like smoke of children passed through fire –

for every falling leaf's a spit
        of flame that wants New England's death
and every leaf's a burning tongue
that cries for vengeance from our wrongs.

The Fall: II. October

The twisted roots begin to stir.
Now mulched with new-born children's soft
unsuckled greenstick bones, they pry
    among the topsoiled Irish graves.
The daughters of dead chambermaids
skip Mass to flirt on Salem's greens.
    New England's gravemuck clogs their feet.
Down, down, the fat roots reach
for bankers' nieces, shy white-bodied
    girls who giggled once out loud
and blushed and fled the bright cotillion;
for Amherst boys, their new mustaches
    wet with ice, who laughed and steamed
and tugged off mittens with their teeth.
Rolled on surging roots, the dead
    Atlantic sailors rise and fall,
the Gloucestermen come safe to shore.
A button on a bright gray shroud,
    a patch of blue, love clasped with grief –
there was a time such things survived,
but now all death is drained of life.
    The cold divines who preached from Kings,
the stone-fence farmers, Mohawk hunters,
pewtersmiths, Green Mountain boys,
    harpooners, poets, crippled bluecoats:
Netted roots have wrapped them round,
sapped them, and plunged deeper down
    toward ancient gulfs where first blood flowed.
At the world's core lies a lake

where slaughters stream and pale roots drink.
    The thick remains of sin are coursing
through October's trees to splatter
red New England's sky with leaves.

The Fall: III. November

> Off Winter Harbor, Christmas Cove,
> Fairhaven, Wellfleet – now the cold
> gray sea turns back against the shore.
> > Hard combers rake between the rocks
> for bottles, paper, bits of glass.
> Angry whitecaps scour the beach
> > and foam among the driftwood dams.
> The signs were there but who believed?
> The long cold grass along the hill
> > stiff with scripts of morning frost,
> the ragged geese-Vs pointing south,
> the rains that splayed the yellow leaves
> > like opened wounds along the path:
> Still the forecast winter stalled
> and we forgot what follows fall.
> > New England's cold November sets
> bare ruined oaks against gray skies.
> A thousand leafless crosses weave
> > among the trees. No hue remains.
> This is the killing time between
> the crime and judgment, act and pain,
> > the pregnant days when we pretend
> that consequences will miscarry –
> witness perjured, time suborned –
> > until at last the winter breaks,
> sweeping down the western hills
> across Vermont, New Hampshire, Maine
> > to fill the valleys, close the woods,
> entomb the cities, still the seas.

Deep in snow New England holds
        lovely, silent, finished, clean.
What mercy after such forgiveness?
What resurrection waits on spring?

The Boston School of Beauty

The beauty school on Brighton Lane
spills pink-smocked girls at twelve o'clock.
They blossom cigarettes and talk,
pluck lilacs from the parish green
and plant them in their hair for spring.
But the bells of St. Columbkille's clang
and Boston mourners dim the street,
with roses on the hearse's seat
to take them to the grave.
And all the novice scissors stop
and all the young beauticians hold
to see the rosewood in the cold
be taken to the grave.
From the flower I hear the bell
the green tongue tolls, and from the swell
of young girls' breasts I hear the sound
that stills the city to the ground
and makes the shurring scissors shut
and stops the lover as he woos.
It's death alone that stays our muse.

The Attic

Before these knot-pocked plywood days,
homespun workmen squared by hand
their shingled gables, ridgepole roofs:
the brute oak centerbeam suspended,
butt-end swung 'round and eyeballed straight,
sledged through the trusses' arms and home
to tie the trestled rafters down.
    In the attic of my father's house
old footprints patter down the joists,
around the bales of cedar shakes,
the decks of warped storm-window frames,
the careful stacks my father made
from cartons of his father's things.
    And here beneath the narrowed eaves,
I set in cautious rows his files,
his ledgers and accounts – as though,
coming down the attic stair
or shutting off the attic light,
I'd hear him calling up to ask
if everything were sealed tight.

Dirge

I should have deadened the street with straw,
I should have stopped the bedroom clock
and stilled the doorbell chimes with crepe,
I should have brought him quinine bark,
exotic simples packed in teak,
I should have had Te Deums sung
with banks of candles, cloistered nuns
to say their beads before he died.
    Before he died, he should have known
his son would hire muffled drums,
his son would shroud his house in black,
he should have known his son would find
the cassocked priests to chant his Mass,
he should have known the raven horse
and sable hearse would trundle past
the silent parks and shuttered shops.
    I should have told him weeping men
would dim the streets like mourning clouds,
I should have knelt beside his bed
and said in life we are in death,
I should have told him sons survive
to keep their father's death alive.

The Undivided Heart
Lines Written on My Daughter Faith's Second Birthday

Why should the aspens shrink from death?
In the clearing after fire,
they sift the sunlight through their leaves:
a ripple shield, a spray of shade
for tender shoots of tower pine
in whose grown shadow aspen dies.

Yesterday I caught my daughter
pushing gently at the mirror,
reaching for her self and other,
learning now that at the heart
of things there is divide. Christ,

it was from this I'd hoped to save her,
shelter her until I died
content beneath her tower shade.

In Faith's green age I climbed the hill
behind the cabin, through the pines,
to sit alone in the fire glade.

The aspens flashed like mirrored panes,
and in the breeze the rippled leaves
whispered there of light and dark,
death and love and sacrifice,
the undivided heart that springs
to fill the broken heart of things.

IV

What Water Washes Wears Away

To us monoglots it may not mean
much of what it used to mean:

> My lover wore my love to sea
> > *What water washes wears away*
> And swore an oath he'd come for me.

Or in some clumsy first construe,
a schoolboy's crib in ancient tongues:

> The poets' golden songs he sang
> > *What water washes wears away*
> And with his vows the foxbells rang.

Who was she who gathered shells
and seaweed wreaths along the strand?

> The violets that are long since dead
> > *What water washes wears away*
> He wove in garlands for my head.

Weak words, to so betray the years,
forgetful tongues, a lover's fears.

> Weak words my lover wore to sea
> > *What water washes wears away*
> But I wait till he comes for me.

Diaspora

On the giant's hill, in the child's eye,
the old house stands hermaphrodite,
the mother-father rolled in light.
In brazen day, that Zion's done:
a trumpet cry to still the sun.

> Beware, my love, beware, beware:
> the sky's on fire and the air
> is singed along its western rim.
> Desire for day at dusk grows dim.

In the city's prism, in the schism light,
the rain bends down the neon night.
Unseen, sequestered daughters cry
and in his bed the young man mourns
the Babylon of traffic horns.

> Cold heart beneath the city street,
> the subway lines, the sewers' heat:
> Cold heart that hates a lovers' twine,
> why break my lover's heart from mine?

In the frozen zero, in the center night,
a cold heart plots against the light
and schemes to hide all glimpse of sky.
The Cities of the Plain will change
my love to salt, her love to strange.

Black Scrawl

The crimson lake that laps her cheek,
her scarlet kiss, her madder hair
once singed the virgin martyr page
but taper down at last to this:
red language, words incarnadine,
black scrawl in sifted ash.

When I have fears that I may cease
to speak beneath my sullen sun
and garner dark at length in day,
then on the shore I stand at night
and hear the constant rollers break,
black wash against the stones.

Words weigh more than words can bear.
No guys, no props, no stays can save
this solid world from solid fall.
Too dense dead stuff – these words, this love:
the rouge on corpses, whited graves,
black shards of broken glass.

Song

I wore, my love, my love to war.
Around my head, for love I wore
the garlands of my love to war,
and brambles from the garden door –
brambles from the garden door.

Heigho, my love, I tore my hair
and caught the briars in my hair.
Heigho, my love, I wore my hair
with touch-me-nots and briars there –
touch-me-nots and briars there.

Beware, my love, my thorny hair.
Beware, my love, the briars there,
and bloody brambles by the door,
and touch-me-nots for love I wore –
touch-me-nots for love I wore.

Tetrameter

Quadruped, the limping line
peers through panes at nursery rhyme.
Doggerel, the hobbled verse
stales against the lilac bush,
and snarls at cymbaled trash-can lids
while snuffling through the garbage bins.
Growling with its withers stiff,
a crippled thing still has to live.

V

Fiat Rex

There being neither bangled dancers
swirling cloth-of-gold and green
nor golden peacocks set in swings
above the garden's marble ponds,
we are assured we are not king.

O, but were I king I would command
my flautists out upon the porch
and golden bowls of tamarinds
and pomegranate seeds in ice
set down within my reach.

Or I would welcome envoys from the East
with feasting and a holiday,
rise to proclaim our love for peace
and whisper orders to proceed.
It's well I do not rule this place

for I would teach the crowded plains
that peace is war in shepherd's dress.
And I would lead great armies south,
and at the Ganges cry aloud
for other worlds to win.

How many died that day in Itaban?
I can't remember but my sword
was black with blood and we won through.
I saw a jackal gnaw a hand
and ordered all the corpses burned.

Now I grow cold and get no heat
from charcoal fires in the spring.
What did it gain? My son is dead
and men put paper in between
my word and deed, and speak of laws,

and I'm an old and heirless king.
I see them smile and look away.
I'll teach them that the old hand still –
I'll summon guards – Antìloches –
no, he's dead these ten years gone;

I do not know if guards will come.
Let Strake and Tolma make their plans
to take this kingdom when I'm gone.
It is enough their fathers stood
beside me while we battled worlds.

I wonder if their ghosts still laugh
at how we broke the Hittites like a dam
and poured our armies on the East.
From the porch, the ivory flutes
ring echoes in the colonnades;

a golden bird's gold feathers trail
down to touch the marble pond.
It's good to sit here and recall,
an old king warming in the sun,
though all the swirling dancers know

we are no king at all.

The Profligate Poet Calls for Bishop Golias

I've seen the seasons drunk with spring
pass out again to fall, and know
that all who wake to summer's song
will sleep again beneath the snow –

And wake again: We're not yet done,
while every sunrise slips her light
beneath old skies set upside down
to turn new cups of day upright.

So come, Golias, though we seem
to teeter on the pagan brink –
Fear not, we'll totter back in time
when faith is strong enough to drink.

Today we'll take the bridegroom's side
and lead him weak-kneed from the nave,
tomorrow take the widow's side
and lead her weeping from the grave.

We'll pledge the spirit's chance occasion:
wine or water, new or old.
And find the purpose in the season:
time to let go, time to hold.

So let us sing, therefore, and dance,
and leave the husk to show what's sown.
There's world enough for sage and dunce.
The only hurry is our own.

The Winter Orchard

Say, my love, this world is whole:
a windfall in the grass beneath the bole.
Or hold, my love, love's time is now:
a flourish, then the fruit along the bough.

But O, my love, how hard to hold
bare thoughts of love in winter's cold.
The empty limbs are bent and gray.
My love, O Christ, my love is far away.

The November Funeral of a Twelve-Year-Old Girl

From faded grass beneath the bole
the last red windfall hunted down,
last marigold, last aster blown,
the dingy shades of autumn fall
and tinctures drown.

The orange-flash gunmen go to ground.
A gray reed takes the wind and sways.
Season of death and fruitlessness:
Green sea-ducks flee the leaden sound
and all tones cease.

Where is the cast of summer's air?
Nothing stays until it's gone.
On that gray day we graved Anne down
the long black hills to dark seas where
dead colors run.

Henry Carter in His Bath
for my godchildren:
Jake Meany, Henry Frank, and Rosemary Crockett

     Reading on the taps the H and C,
he thought how sweet this world must be
to mark for every boy a tub
with towels afterwards to rub.
     Henry, you mistake much less
than men with more from which to guess.
Though things aren't always as they read,
when all is written, still we need
each of us to find our tub
and towels afterwards to rub.

Larvatus Prodeo

(In the fall of 1630, René Descartes wrote a series of extrava-
gantly quarrelsome letters to the Dutch mathematician Isaac
Beeckman, accusing him of plagiarizing a treatise on music
written but left unpublished by Descartes twelve years before.
Larvatus prodeo, "I go forth masked," is the curious description
Descartes gives of his own publications.)

      Everyday, my erstwhile friend,
I think to hear you've met your end
dangling down some scaffold's rope.
Still, you mustn't lose your hope
in Our Lord's mercy: Just recall
the first of men to sit with all
the Holy Angels was a thief,
and pray you find a like relief.
      But you will note my tone is light,
for though I know to praise the right
and blame the wrong, I do not fault
the mad for what they cannot halt.
And what but madness made you rake
my trash for something you could take
and, seeing glitter, think to find
something bright enough to blind?
Frenchmen do not throw out gold
nor call the thief of refuse bold.
      Yet I here set aside complaint
to tell you that your lost restraint
marks no gain among the wise:
a published author we despise.
As painters paint themselves in frame,
he's caught by letters in his name.

Why marvel when his readers look
more for the man than for his book?
        Better to do as the poet bid:
Living well, we must be well hid.
I tell you though you have not asked,
when I go forth, I go forth masked.

VI

Twelve Quatrains

1. Luring, Shunning, Fetching, Running

Luring, shunning, fetching, running,
she plies her love in feint attack.
Thirsty drowning, clothed ungowning,
she tenders love to take love back.

2. The Discipline of Classics

Subject, object, gender, verb –
a second lesson did I serve:
how even schooled men fall to fools
while teaching Greek to pretty girls.

3. What Water Washes Wears Away

I wrote my name upon the water
with a stick on Boston's bay
and caught up in my arms my daughter.
What water washes wears away.

4. Old Hat

Vicky's lascivious anti-Victorian
story appeared in the latest review.
Vicky, supposing she'll shock the censorious,
shocks by supposing that shocking is new.

5. On Furrowed Seas

On furrowed seas past unplowed gulfs
she drove our love down the tempest's throat
where words like white-capped waves would rage
and raise their heads to storm love's boat.

6. The Trial

The gentle rains refused to judge,
excused in pardoned murmurs love.
But as I turned my collar up,
the thunder's verdict stormed above.

7. *The Assistant Professor's Malediction*

This curse against the Dean I write:
May your sons dig your grave by night,
as I engrave these lines about
your sudden death – and scratch them out.

8. *The Living Rule*

The living rule, the holy nun,
awaits her Savior in the sun,
and when the sun puts out her light,
awaits her Savior in the night.

9. *Dead Kings*

Dead kings may scrabble at their lids
and heroes curse the day they fell
but if our graves are cut to fit
we smaller men should wear death well.

10. Dickinsonesque

The Whip does not refuse – to Scourge –
The Beaten Man – to Moan –
Each its Proper Use – Enjoins –
He Flails – my Heart – Unknown –

11. Heloise on Abelard

Though he sounds no trumpet in the hall,
there's still some triumph in our fall:
All love is perfect in the heart;
only its instruments fail their part.

12. Flint in Water

Flint in water, steel in flame,
and adamant in blood will melt.
But she is harder than them all:
my burning tears, my wounds unfelt.

Modern Catholic Verse

(A review of *Place of Passage: Contemporary Catholic Poetry*, ed.
David Craig and Janet McCann [Story Line Press, 2000])

David Craig and Janet McCann
(he teaches at Steubenville, does what he can;
she writes for *America*, also *McCall's*)
lead off their book with some work of John Paul's.
  That's the pope, as you know, which gives them some force
to start *Place of Passage*, their volume of verse
by "contemporary Catholics" to sound through the ages.
Sixty-four poets will fill up their pages.
  There's Murray Bodo, Adelia Prado,
Impastato, Marcello, and Carolyn Alessio.
There's Sarah Appleton, Sean Brendan-Brown,
Marion, Pelton, and monk Thomas Merton.
  Feela and Gioia, Murray and Yanity,
Mariani, Muratori, Lynskey, and Ande.
Robert McDowell, Jeremy Driscoll,
Russell and Mistral, a poet named Knoepfle.
  Oh, and did I mention the pope?
But don't let the contents-page raise too much hope,
for it's after John Paul that things start to get worse:
There aren't enough Catholics writing good verse.
  "Contemporary," I thought, means just "today."
It makes you wonder if old Claude McKay
knew when he died more than fifty years back
that Craig and McCann would dig him up for their claque?
  Mistral, Fitzgerald, though here, aren't alive.
Levertov, Merton, too, don't survive.
But you can't make a book of just new Catholics good.
If David and Janet can't do it, who could?

"There are many things in our lives that are burnished"
(they write in the intro. with which the book's furnished)
"by their use in church" – that's intended as prose,
but in *Place of Passage*, what poet still knows
    his poems from prosings, his crystal from isinglass?
"Let me mention one or two things about Christmas,"
demands Annie Dillard. "Of course, you've all beard . . . ."
(I'll bet even-money that's supposed to be "heard."

    Still, it sounds rather stolid, so maybe the line
is one of those touches by which poets define
their distinction from second-rate writers of prose.)
The political odes take a left-leaning pose:
    "The Catholic mythology" must include in its run
"the lonely figure in the jungle and the . . . militant nun,"
say Craig and McCann. It's really quite weird –
but then poets can nod (as I'm sure you've all beard.)

    "Banditos in the canyon," opines poet Knoepfle,
"banditos in the boardroom" – isn't it awful?
You'd think even bad Catholic bards would be bright.
But if David and Janet can't find them, who might?

    "*Ich ruf zu dir*," Frank Stewart must shout
when from "inside the . . . storage . . . alfalfa" comes out.
Bruce Dawe's deep in love "with a girl" he calls "Life."
She's spooky, mysterious, bad for a wife.
    Or take Robert Lax's odd verbal run:
"one bird / two birds / three birds / one."
That's half the whole poem. It's called just "(one bird)."
(The parens are important; note the way that they gird.)
    No one called "Bottum" has power to pun
on someone's last name – but isn't it fun?

When David and Janet say "Lax" is a "part
of that old Merton gang," it wrenches the heart.
    While I read *Place of Passage* in slow, easy stages,
I found myself scrawling some notes on the pages
like "Just when you thought that things couldn't get worse,
along come collections of new Catholic verse."
    But such comment's unfair. Just a fraction –
"faith's a tide, . . . ebbs and flows, . . . / action . . . inaction" –
of Levertov is worth any number of lurches,
or Richard Smith's rage at the syncretist churches,
    or that "Prayer for the Harvest" of Robert McDowell's,
or most of Les Murray's Australian growls.
The "canon of possessions," D. Gioia sings,
is only dispossessing: "a litany of lost things."
    But most of this work is not good and not bad.
It's just pious and worthy and terribly sad.
These editors can't be dismissed as mere fools,
but no workman succeeds with inferior tools.
    If David and Janet (Craig and McCann)
can't do it, then who of us possibly can?

On Publishing His Memoirs

The confidences of my lovers
Were bound to end between these covers.

The Kiln

On the wheel, there's room to mend,
adjust these lines, erase the rings.
After fire, ends remain: to break or shelve,
wet more clay, and start again.
      Though I have been Savonarola to myself
and burnt my vanities in fright,
no clay was fired in those flames
but only broken bits of light.
      These are neither words nor things:
the friar in his fever, the stoker on his height
burn to watch the fire burning
even through the night.

The Feet Like Water

The feet like water washed the slate
and eased the edges of these stairs.
Flowing hands shellacked the brick
and lapped the open ceiling beams
with eddies from their cigarettes.
We are the stream of old intent,
the current in the places left

On an Ancient Roman Frieze

This broidered graven scene ingrains
      the moral habit. Work is weighed
           in beauty's balance, scruple's scales:
                  carved and carved away, the same.
                  Deliberate, the sculptors came
           to liberate the stone details,
      but scrupulous in what they made,
balance with the stone remains.

VII

Washington, D.C., the First of May

Walking alone around the new-mown
Dupont Circle – where she once laughed
at falling leaves and turned to ask
how long we'd be till we moved West –
I know the time for change has passed.
Leave the long-dead Wobblies resting
still beside the Spanish Brigades.
We who are left are all too tired:
unorganized, splintered, alone,
dismayed.

Heading east down Massachusetts
half a mile to Fourteenth Street,
I could – if she had stayed till spring –
show her the buildings burned in '68,
machine guns on the White House lawn,
and demonstrate how things went wrong.
Cripple Creek and Comstock, too,
Lawrence, Massachusetts:
The unions struck and burned too soon.
We know more now than those men knew.

Riding on the Red Line back
to Dupont Station, I have thought
on driving West for some return
of all the things her leaving turned.
My mind has run on setting out to find
the cottonwoods that Captain Lewis
camped beneath one early spring
waiting for Clark to come upstream,
Big Bill Haywood's missing home,
or Joe Hill's mountain grave.

Walking again around the Circle –
where she had danced through yellow leaves –
I watch the cleanup crews begin
to clear the dead growth left from fall
and bank the chips around the trees.
This year they've left the fountain off.
From the gray-leaf mulch the furls
of red-flagged tulips flicker down
like dying flames among the ashes,
like broken marchers filing home.

Hades' Lament at Persephone's Annual Departure

And she said
How
She said
Put it back
Put it back
Put it
On the back burner
For a while.
The back
Burn
Back burner
And she said
How
She said
Put it
Back
Put it
Back
Put it
On the back burner
For a while.

Hymeneal

This is the cause of darkness,
that the stars move away from their light.
That a son must leave his father's house,
this is the cause of night.

And this is the cause of daybreak,
that the dawn turns back from its night.
That you brought me home from the homeless dark,
this is the cause of light.

St. Columbkille's

Extra ecclesiam non salus

Boston's lovers do not mind
winter's blast against their kind.
They bring their sleds down Market Street
or steal trays from Taco Bell
to show off for the Irish girls
and sleigh them down the parish hill.
      From my window down the street
I hear the banging parish bell.
I brush away the ash that fell,
and light another cigarette.
      I've got the cancer in my throat
that leaves no voice to tell
how lovers slide down winter's hill
and are not saved by poets' skill.

Love in Boston

The college girls wore black this spring,
army camouflage and green
and the kind of high-top sneaks
Bob Cousy wore to play the Knicks.
　　　　I asked them why they dressed this way,
but *Love is dead* is all they'd say.

The driver said, *I hit a rock*
but before I could get out and look
the businessmen
had looted all the flowers from my van.
You don't look for that from men in suits.
　　　　It's love has made my sisters mutes
and taken all the order from their lives.
Their husbands took bright muses for their wives
but in the city late most nights
they wander their apartments dousing lights
or watch the local TV crews
film disgruntled florists for the news.

The gardener says they have no cause,
these patches on the Harvard Lawn,
and roses disappear at dawn
from trellises along the walls.
　　　　Used to be, he said, *it'd be the boys,*
stealing flowers, making noise
over across at Radcliffe's halls.
But nothing makes these new kids run.
Back last fall, before she died,
she laughed, my wife, until she cried,
when I told her they say love's been done.

The doctors whisper down the hall.
The night nurse leans her head against the wall
and lets the patients ring.
She'd heard that afternoon her daughter sing
a song she'd learned in nursery school.
She won't let love make her a fool
the way it made her mother one.
She'll grow up bright, and tall, and cool,
and find a man, or maybe none,
or maybe that won't matter, once she's grown.

My mother and her sisters give
piano lessons in the day.
Their students never learn to play
but only to regret.
God, I wish that I were deaf
or had the music in my hands –
the living rule that can remake
the sounds we hear that others make.
I'd shape a world without a fall
with roses trellised on the wall
and gardens where it's always spring:
Perfection matched to will as eye to light,
and love to love as dark to night
or age to death's ingathering.

And if there were a stone on Beacon Hill
where I could stand, blaspheme, and die,
would she hold me there, lie still,
brush back my hair and cry?

In Refusal of Politics
Sapphics for RJN

If I have seen geese low on the east horizon,
seen the long reeds strain in the dawn to follow,
watched the first clean ice of the season take
roots for the winter,

what worth are those hard scenes in a day that fathers
lunge at half-born sons with a knife, and daughters
name the swift-gained deaths of their mothers high
gestures of mercy?

And they that speak strong words in the failing season,
stoking new fires, cursing the embers – they must
scorn the faint hearts nursing a private flame,
skirting the darkness.

But still the cold reeds sway in the wind and whisper:
Leave the great voice raging to stave the winter.
Autumn's own soft music has need of songs,
gentle and dying.

About the Author

Joseph Bottum is Books & Arts editor of the *Weekly Standard* in Washington, D.C. A native of South Dakota, he is a graduate of Georgetown University, with a Ph.D. in medieval philosophy from Boston College. In addition to his duties at the *Weekly Standard*, he is poetry editor of the journal *First Things* and host of "Book Talk," a nationally syndicated radio program. His writing has appeared in the *Atlantic Monthly*, the *Wall Street Journal*, *Nineteenth-Century Literature*, *Commentary*, *Philosophy and Literature*, the *Wilson Quarterly*, and many other newspapers, magazines, and journals.